Big and Small

By Jim Pipe

Aladdin/Watts

London • Sydney

Big

Eddie is at the park.
What is big?

The trees in the park
are big. Is this tree as
big as an elephant?

2

Some trees are very big. But that building is even bigger!

Small

What is small?

A mouse is small, and so is the butterfly on Eddie's head!

This bug is very small. It is tiny.
It can walk around on a leaf.

Big and small

Here are two ducks.

One is big, and one is small,

like Eddie's teddies!

Here are some leaves. Which are big and which are small?

Big or small

Sometimes Eddie feels big.

He acts like a big gorilla!

Sometimes Eddie feels small.

He needs help to get a drink.

Bigger and smaller

Eddie plays with a football and a tennis ball. Which is bigger?

The football is bigger. It is as big as a melon!

10

A balloon starts off small.

But it gets bigger and bigger!

Biggest and smallest

Dogs can be big or small, just like people. Which dog is biggest and which is smallest?

The biggest dog is brown and white. It walks up to Eddie.

The smallest dog is black and white. It takes Eddie's ball!

Growing

What grows bigger?

Children grow and so do plants. Soon this flower will be bigger than Eddie.

Animals grow, too. One day these puppies will be as big as their mum!

Getting smaller

What gets smaller?

Eddie's ice cream gets smaller and smaller, like a melting candle.

What else gets smaller?

A jumper that shrinks in the wash gets smaller!

Near and far

What looks smaller?

Near to Eddie, the boats look big.
Far away, they look smaller.

A plane is very big close up.
In the sky it looks tiny!

Sizes

It is time to go home.

Mum's bike is too big for Eddie.

This one is too small.

Eddie's bike is just right!

Goodbye!

Here are some words about size.

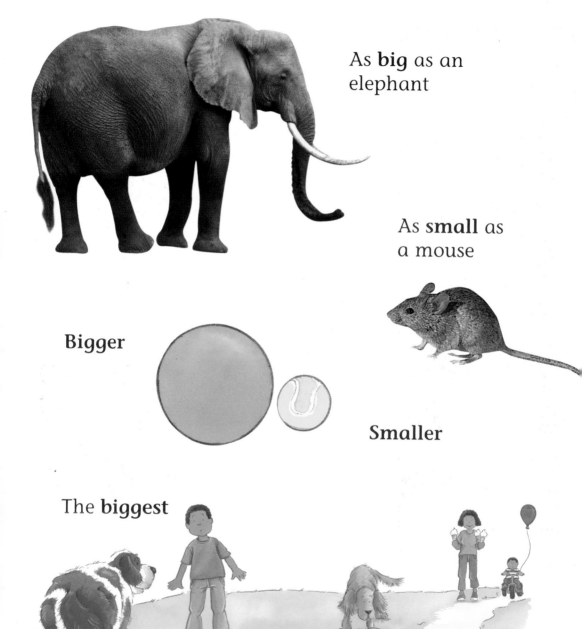

As **big** as an elephant

As **small** as a mouse

Bigger

Smaller

The **biggest**

The **smallest**

Here are some big and small things.

Bug

Bicycle

Leaves

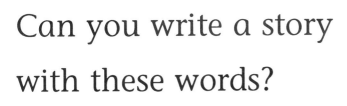

Building

Flower

Can you write a story
with these words?

Do you know?

Is it big or small?

Here are three ways to find out.

Weigh it.

Measure it.

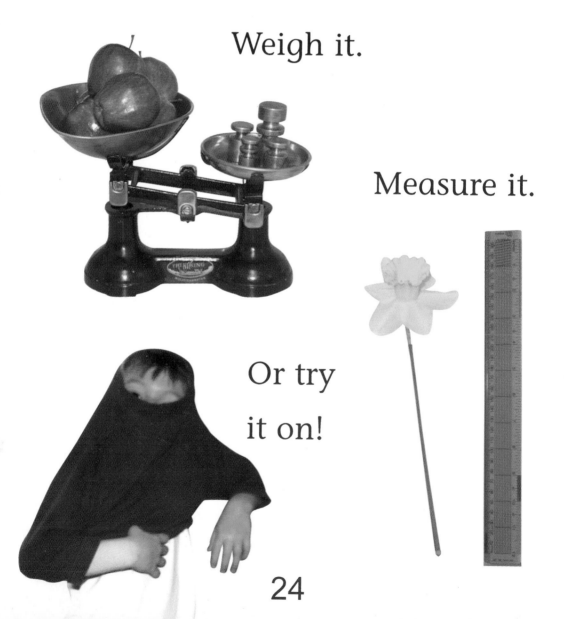

Or try
it on!